THE ULTIMATE INTERVIEW PREP GUIDE

Mastering the Most Common Interview
Questions to Land Your Dream Job

ROBERT L. MARK

Copyright

All rights reserved. No part of this publication **The Ultimate Interview Prep Guide** may be reproduced, stored in a retrieval system or transmitted in any form or by any means, electronic, mechanical, photocopying, recording, scanning, without written permission from the publisher or author, except as permitted by U.S copyright law

Printed in the United State of America

© 2024 by Robert L. Mark

Who Needs This Book

Are you a new graduate stepping into the job market, a seasoned professional considering a career shift, or someone returning to work after a break? This book offers essential insights and strategies to excel in any interview. Filled with practical tips, frequently asked interview questions, and expert advice on showcasing yourself with confidence and clarity, "The Ultimate Interview Prep Guide" is the ideal resource for anyone determined to secure their dream job.

About the Author

Robert Mark is an acclaimed career coach and with over 15 years of experience in recruitment and career development, Robert has helped thousands of individuals navigate the complexities of job interviews. His expertise lies in providing practical strategies and insights that empower job seekers to present their best selves confidently. Robert's passion for helping others succeed in their careers is evident in his engaging writing style and comprehensive approach, making "The Ultimate Interview Prep Guide" an indispensable resource for anyone looking to land their dream job.

Contents

Copyright ii

Who Needs This Book iii

About the Author iv

Contents v

Introduction 1

    Welcome to Your Job Search Journey 1

    Understanding the Importance of Interview Preparation 1

    How This Book Will Help You Succeed 6

Chapter 1: Preparing for the Interview 11

    Researching the Company 11

    Understanding the Job Description 15

    Knowing Your Resume 18

Chapter 2: The Basics of Interviewing 22

    First Impressions Matter 22

    Dress Code and Professional Appearance 22

    Punctuality and Preparation 24

    Body Language and Communication Skills 26

    The Role of Voice and Tone 31

    Active RESUME Listening 33

Chapter 3: Common Interview Questions 36

    Tell Me About Yourself 36

    What Are Your Strengths and Weaknesses? 39

Why Do You Want to Work with Us? 42
Chapter 4: Behavioral Interview Questions 45
　STAR Method: Situation, Task, Action, Result 45
　Tell Me About a Time You Faced a Challenge 48
　Describe a Successful Project You Managed 49
Chapter 5: Technical and Job-Specific Questions 52
　Preparing for Technical Questions 52
　Demonstrating Your Industry Knowledge 54
Chapter 6: Questions to Ask the Interviewer 57
　Making a Lasting Impression 57
　Evaluating the Company Culture 63
Chapter 7: Handling Difficult Questions 68
　Addressing Employment Gaps 68
　Discussing Salary Expectations 73
Chapter 8: Follow-Up and Next Steps 75
　Post-Interview Etiquette 75
　Handling Rejections and Offers 77
Chapter 9: Special Situations 81
　Group Interviews and Assessment Centers 81
　Remote and Virtual Interviews 83
Chapter 10: Continuing Your Career Growth 86
　Building Professional Growth 86
　Lifelong Learning and Development 89
　Your Path to Success 92

Sample Interview Questions and Answers 99

Model Answers From Professionals 101

    Responses from a Software Developer 101

    Responses from a Customer Representive Role . 110

    Responses from a Professional Nurse 120

    Responses from an Academic 129

    Responses from an Operation Manager 138

Introduction

Welcome to Your Job Search Journey

Welcome to your job search journey! This is an exciting and important step in your career, and understanding how to navigate it effectively can make all the difference. Whether you are just starting out or looking to make a change, being well-prepared can help you stand out and achieve your goals. This introduction will guide you through the importance of interview preparation and how this book will assist you in succeeding.

Understanding the Importance of Interview Preparation

Preparing for an interview is crucial for several reasons. Let's break it down into key points to understand why it's so important.

1. First Impressions Matter

The interview is often the first time you meet your potential employer face-to-face or virtually. Making a good first impression is critical because it sets the tone for the rest of the interview. This includes how you dress, your body language, and how you communicate. Being well-prepared helps you present yourself confidently and professionally.

2. Demonstrating Your Skills and Qualifications:

Interviews are your chance to showcase your skills, experience, and qualifications. It's not just about listing what you have done, but demonstrating how your experiences make you the right fit for the job. Preparation allows you to articulate your thoughts clearly and provide specific examples that highlight your strengths.

3. Understanding the Company:

Employers appreciate candidates who have done their homework. Knowing about the company's history, values, culture, and recent achievements shows that you are genuinely interested in the position. This knowledge helps you tailor your answers to align with the company's goals and culture.

4. Answering Common Questions Confidently:

Many interview questions are predictable, such as "Tell me about yourself," "Why do you want to work here?" or "What are your strengths and weaknesses?" Being prepared for these questions allows you to respond confidently and avoid being caught off guard. Practicing your answers helps you to be concise and focused.

5. Handling Unexpected Questions:

Even with the best preparation, you might face unexpected questions. Being prepared helps you stay calm and think on your feet. If you have practiced your responses and know your resume inside out, you can adapt your answers to suit the question, showing your problem-solving skills and adaptability.

6. Showcasing Your Personality:

Interviews are not just about skills and experience; they are also about personality. Employers want to know if you will fit into their team and work environment. Preparation helps you to be yourself and let your personality shine through in a positive way.

7. Asking Intelligent Questions:

Towards the end of the interview, you will likely be asked if you have any questions. This is your opportunity to learn more about the company and the role, and to show that you are seriously considering the position. Preparing questions in advance demonstrates your enthusiasm and critical thinking.

8. Reducing Anxiety:

Interviewing can be nerve-wracking, especially if it's for a job you really want. Preparation helps reduce anxiety because you know you have done everything possible to be ready. This confidence can help you perform better and leave a lasting positive impression.

9. Learning from Experience:

Each interview is a learning experience. By preparing thoroughly, you can evaluate what went well and what could be improved after each interview. This continuous improvement makes you better with each interview you attend.

10. Increasing Your Chances of Success:

Ultimately, preparation increases your chances of getting the job. Employers can tell when a candidate has put in the effort to prepare, and it often makes the difference between getting hired and being overlooked.

How This Book Will Help You Succeed
This book is designed to be your comprehensive guide to job search success. Here's how it will help you achieve your goals:

1. Step-by-Step Guidance:

The book provides a clear, step-by-step process for preparing for interviews and the overall job search journey. Each chapter focuses on a specific aspect, from resume writing to interview techniques, making it easy to follow and implement.

2. Practical Tips and Strategies:

You will find practical tips and strategies that you can apply immediately. These include how to research a company, how to dress for an interview, and how to answer tough questions. The book aims to be a practical resource that you can refer to whenever you need it.

3. Real-Life Examples:

To help you understand the concepts better, the book includes real-life examples and case studies. These examples illustrate how successful candidates have navigated their job searches and interviews, providing you with inspiration and ideas.

4. Interactive Exercises:

The book is not just about reading; it's also about doing. Interactive exercises and practice questions help you apply what you've learned.

These exercises are designed to build your confidence and ensure you are well-prepared.

5. Expert Advice:

The book is written by experts in the field of career coaching and recruitment. You will benefit from their years of experience and insider knowledge, giving you an edge over other candidates.

6. Common Pitfalls to Avoid:

It's easy to make mistakes in the job search process. The book highlights common pitfalls and how to avoid them. This includes everything from avoiding generic resumes to not following up after an interview. Knowing these pitfalls helps you navigate the process smoothly.

7. Building a Professional Network:

The book emphasizes the importance of networking and provides tips on how to build and maintain a professional network. Networking can open doors to opportunities that are not advertised and can give you valuable insights into companies and industries.

8. Tailoring Your Approach:

Every job and company is different, and a one-size-fits-all approach doesn't work. The book teaches you how to tailor your resume, cover letter, and interview responses to each specific job. This customization increases your chances of standing out and getting noticed.

9. Long-Term Career Planning:

Beyond just getting a job, the book helps you think about your long-term career goals. It guides you on how to choose the right job that aligns with your career aspirations and provides advice on career development and growth.

10. Confidence Building:

One of the key outcomes of reading this book is increased confidence. By knowing what to expect and how to prepare, you will feel more confident in your abilities and your chances of success. Confidence is often the deciding factor in whether you get the job.

Chapter 1: Preparing for the Interview

Preparing for an interview can be a daunting task, but with the right approach, it becomes manageable and even enjoyable. In this chapter, we'll break down the preparation process into three main sections: Researching the Company, understanding the Job Description, and Knowing Your Resume.

Each section will cover important points to ensure you are thoroughly prepared for your interview.

Researching the Company

Understanding the company you are interviewing with is crucial. It shows that you are genuinely interested in the role and the organization. Here are the key areas to focus on when researching a company:

Understanding the Company's Mission and Values

The mission and values of a company are its guiding principles. They represent what the company stands for and strives to achieve. Here's how you can understand them:

1. Visit the Company's Website: Start by visiting the company's official website. Look for sections like "About Us," "Our Mission," or "Core Values." These sections often provide a clear overview of the company's goals and principles.

2. Read Annual Reports and Press Releases: These documents can offer insights into the company's achievements and how they align with their mission. Annual reports are typically available on the company's website.

3. Social Media and Blogs: Follow the company on social media platforms like

LinkedIn, Twitter, and Facebook. Companies often share their values and culture through posts and blogs.

4. Understanding Alignment: Once you know the company's mission and values, think about how they align with your own values and career goals. Be prepared to discuss this alignment during the interview, as it shows you are a good cultural fit for the company.

Analyzing Recent News and Developments

Staying updated on the latest news about the company can give you a competitive edge. Here's how you can analyze recent news and developments:

1. News Websites and Industry Publications: Regularly check news websites and industry-specific publications for articles about the company. Websites like Bloomberg, Reuters, and industry blogs are good sources.

2. Google News Alerts: Set up Google News Alerts for the company's name. This way, you'll receive updates directly in your email whenever the company is mentioned in the news.

3. Company Press Releases: Check the company's press release section on their website. This section will have official announcements about new products, partnerships, or other significant events.

4. Social Media Updates: Companies often share news and updates on their social media profiles. Follow these profiles to stay informed about their latest activities.

5. Analyzing Impact: Reflect on how these developments might impact the company's future. Think about how your role could contribute to these new directions or help the company overcome any challenges mentioned in the news.

Understanding the Job Description

Thoroughly understanding the job description is essential to ensure you are a good fit for the role and to prepare effectively for the interview. Here's how you can break down the job description:

Key Responsibilities and Required Skills

1. Identify Key Responsibilities: Carefully read through the job description and highlight the main responsibilities. These are the tasks you will be expected to perform regularly.

For example, if you're applying for a marketing manager position, key responsibilities might include developing marketing strategies, managing social media campaigns, and analyzing market trends.

2. List Required Skills: Make a list of the skills required for the job. These can be hard skills

(like proficiency in certain software) or soft skills (like communication or teamwork).

For example, a software developer position required skills might include programming languages like Java or Python, problem-solving abilities, and teamwork.

3. Understand Priorities: Some job descriptions mention "preferred" skills in addition to required ones. Pay attention to these as well, as they can give you an edge over other candidates.

4. Research Job Functions: If some responsibilities or skills are unfamiliar, research them to understand what they entail. Use resources like job function guides or industry-specific websites.

Aligning Your Skills with the Job Requirements

1. Match Your Skills: Compare the list of required skills and responsibilities with your

own skills and experiences. Identify areas where you match and where you might need to up skill.

2. Highlight Relevant Experience: Think about specific experiences from your past jobs, education, or volunteer work that align with the key responsibilities of the job. Prepare to discuss these in the interview.

3. Skill Gaps: Identify any skill gaps and think about how you can address them. Are there any short courses or certifications you can take? Are there similar experiences you can highlight that demonstrate your ability to learn quickly?

4. Prepare Examples: Prepare specific examples that demonstrate your skills and experience. Use the STAR method (Situation, Task, Action, and Result) to structure your

answers. This method helps you provide clear and concise responses.

For example, if a key responsibility is managing a team, think of a time when you successfully led a team project. Describe the situation, your task, the actions you took, and the results of your efforts.

Knowing Your Resume
Knowing your resume inside out is critical. It's your personal story and primary tool for showcasing your qualifications. Here's how you can prepare:

Highlighting Relevant Experience

1. Review Your Resume: Go through your resume line by line. Make sure you can discuss every point in detail if asked.

2. Focus on Relevance: Identify the most relevant experiences and achievements related

to the job you're applying for. Be ready to elaborate on these points during the interview.

For example, if you're applying for a sales position, highlight your experience in achieving sales targets, your customer relationship management skills, and any sales awards you have received.

3. Quantify Achievements: Where possible, quantify your achievements. Numbers make your accomplishments more tangible and impressive.

For example, instead of saying, "Increased sales," say, "Increased sales by 20% over six months by implementing a new customer outreach strategy."

4. Tailor Your Story: Think about how each experience has prepared you for the new role. Be ready to connect your past roles with the

responsibilities of the job you are interviewing for.

Preparing to Discuss Gaps and Transitions

1. Identify Gaps: Look for any gaps in your employment history. Be honest with yourself about why these gaps exist.

2. Craft Honest Explanations: Prepare honest and concise explanations for these gaps. Focus on what you did during these periods, such as any learning, volunteering, or personal projects.

For example, if you took a gap year to travel, you might explain how this time helped you develop independence and cultural awareness.

3. Highlight Transitions: Think about any major career transitions you've made. Be ready to explain why you made these changes and how they have prepared you for this role.

For example, if you transitioned from a technical role to a managerial one, explain how your technical background gives you a unique perspective as a manager.

4. Address Concerns: Be prepared for follow-up questions about gaps and transitions. Employers might be concerned about job stability or commitment. Reassure them by emphasizing your skills and how they are suited to the role you're applying for.

Chapter 2: The Basics of Interviewing

First Impressions Matter

First impressions are crucial in every interview, as they can significantly influence your success. Here are some ways to make a positive first impression on a hiring manager:

Dress Code and Professional Appearance

During an interview. Your appearance is one of the first things an interviewer notices about you, and it can significantly influence their perception. Dressing appropriately for an interview demonstrates respect for the company and the interviewer, and it can boost your confidence.

1. Understanding the Dress Code

Every company has a unique culture, and their expectations for dress code can vary widely. Here are some common types of dress codes:

- Business Formal: This is the most conservative type of dress code. It usually includes a suit and tie for men and a pantsuit or skirt suit for women. Colors should be muted, such as black, navy, or gray.
- Business Casual: This is less formal but still professional. Men might wear dress slacks or khakis with a collared shirt, and women might wear a blouse with slacks or a skirt. Jackets are optional.
- Casual: Some modern workplaces have a casual dress code, which might include jeans and a nice shirt. However, even in a casual environment, it's best to dress a bit more formally for an interview.

2. Choosing Your Outfit
- Research the Company: Look at the company's website or social media profiles to get a sense of their dress

code. If you know someone who works there, ask them about the dress code.

- Err on the Side of Formality: If you're unsure, it's better to be slightly overdressed than underdressed. A polished appearance shows that you take the interview seriously.
- Pay Attention to Details: Make sure your clothes are clean, ironed, and fit well. Avoid flashy accessories or strong fragrances, as these can be distracting.

Punctuality and Preparation

Being punctual and prepared is crucial for making a positive first impression. It shows that you are responsible, respectful of other people's time, and serious about the opportunity. When you arrive on time for an interview, you will gain the following advantages:

- Respect for the Interviewer: Arriving on time shows that you value the interviewer's time and the opportunity they are providing.
- Demonstrates Reliability: Punctuality is a key indicator of reliability. If you can't arrive on time for an interview, the interviewer might question your ability to be punctual in the job itself.
- Reduces Stress: Arriving early gives you time to relax, review your notes, and mentally prepare, reducing anxiety and helping you perform better.
- Plan Your Route: Know exactly where you're going and how long it will take to get there. Use a map or navigation app to find the best route.

Body Language and Communication Skills
Maintaining Eye Contact

Eye contact is a powerful form of non-verbal communication. It conveys confidence, attentiveness, and honesty. Here's why maintaining eye contact is important during an interview and how to do it effectively:

Maintaining eye contact with the interviewer offers several benefits.

- Builds Connection: Making eye contact helps you connect with the interviewer, making the conversation feel more personal and engaging.
- Conveys Confidence: Steady eye contact shows that you are confident and self-assured. Avoiding eye contact can make you appear nervous or evasive.
- Demonstrates Attentiveness: It indicates that you are paying attention and

interested in what the interviewer is saying.

How to Maintain Appropriate Eye Contact

1. Balanced Approach: Aim to maintain eye contact about 60-70% of the time. Too much eye contact can be intense or uncomfortable, while too little can seem disinterested.

2. Natural Movements: Let your eye contact be natural. You can look away briefly to think or take notes, but always return to making eye contact.

3. Practice: Practice maintaining eye contact in everyday conversations to become more comfortable with it. You can also practice in front of a mirror or with a friend.

Using Positive Body Language

Your body language can communicate as much, if not more, than your words. Positive body language helps to reinforce what you are saying and creates a favorable impression. The following are the key elements of positive body language.

1. Posture: Sit up straight but not rigid. A good posture conveys confidence and professionalism. Avoid slouching, as it can make you appear uninterested or unmotivated.

2. Gestures: Use natural hand gestures to emphasize points, but avoid excessive or distracting movements. Keep your gestures open and relaxed.

3. Facial Expressions: Smile genuinely and appropriately. A friendly expression can make you seem more approachable and enthusiastic. Avoid frowning or looking overly serious.

4. Nodding: Nodding occasionally when the interviewer is speaking shows that you are listening and engaged in the conversation.

How to be good at Positive Body Language

1. Record Yourself: Record a mock interview and review your body language. Look for areas where you can improve, such as avoiding crossing your arms or fidgeting.

2. Seek Feedback: Practice with a friend or mentor who can provide constructive feedback on your body language.

3. Stay Relaxed: The more relaxed you are, the more natural your body language will be. Take deep breaths, and remind yourself to stay calm.

4. Maintain Eye Contact: Consistent eye contact shows that you are engaged and attentive. It helps build trust and connection with others.

5. Smile Genuinely: A sincere smile can make you appear friendly and approachable, creating a positive impression.

6. Adopt an Open Posture: Keep your body relaxed and open. Avoid crossing your arms or legs, as these can appear defensive or closed-off.

7. Use Gestures Purposefully: Incorporate natural and deliberate hand movements to emphasize your points, but avoid excessive or distracting gestures.

8. Lean In Slightly: When someone is speaking to you, lean in a bit to show interest and attentiveness. This subtle cue indicates that you are fully engaged in the conversation.

9. Mirror the Other Person: Subtly mimic the body language of the person you are interacting with. This can create a sense of rapport and understanding.

10. Keep Your Hands Visible: Keeping your hands out of your pockets and in view demonstrates openness and honesty.

11. Nod to Show Agreement: Nod occasionally while listening to show that you are following along and agree with what is being said.

12. Maintain Good Posture: Stand or sit up straight to convey confidence and authority. Avoid slouching, which can appear unprofessional or uninterested.

13. Be Mindful of Facial Expressions: Ensure that your facial expressions match the tone and content of the conversation. This alignment enhances communication and conveys sincerity.

The Role of Voice and Tone
Your voice and tone are critical components of communication. They can convey enthusiasm, confidence, and clarity, helping to reinforce the

content of your message. The following are the tips for effective vocal communication.

1. Clear and Steady: Speak clearly and at a moderate pace. Avoid speaking too quickly, which can make you difficult to understand, or too slowly, which can make you seem uncertain.

2. Variety in Tone: Use variations in your tone to emphasize important points and keep the listener engaged. A monotone voice can be dull and uninteresting.

3. Volume: Ensure your voice is loud enough to be heard comfortably, but not so loud that it seems aggressive. Adjust your volume based on the setting and the distance between you and the interviewer.

4. Pausing: Don't be afraid to pause briefly to gather your thoughts. This can make your answers more deliberate and impactful.

Practicing Your Vocal Delivery

- Read Aloud: Practice reading aloud to improve your clarity and pacing. Record yourself and listen to identify areas for improvement.
- Mock Interviews: Conduct mock interviews with friends or mentors, focusing on your vocal delivery. Ask for feedback on your tone, volume, and clarity.
- Breathing Exercises: Practice deep breathing exercises to help control your nerves and maintain a steady, calm voice.

Active Listening

Active listening is an essential skill in an interview. It involves fully focusing on the interviewer, understanding their questions, and responding thoughtfully. The following are the components of active listening.

1. Full Attention: Give the interviewer your full attention. Avoid distractions and focus on what they are saying.

2. Clarifying Questions: If you don't understand a question, ask for clarification. This shows that you are engaged and want to provide a relevant answer.

3. Reflective Responses: Reflect on what the interviewer has said before responding. This demonstrates that you are considering their words carefully.

How to practicing Active Listening

1. Mindfulness Exercises: Practice mindfulness to improve your ability to stay present and focused during conversations.

2. Note-Taking: Take brief notes during the interview to help you remember key points and demonstrate your attentiveness.

3. Feedback Loop: Repeat or paraphrase the interviewer's questions or comments to ensure understanding and show that you are listening.

Chapter 3: Common Interview Questions

Tell Me About Yourself
Crafting a Concise and Engaging Narrative

When an interviewer asks, "Tell me about yourself," they are not looking for your entire life story. Instead, they want a brief and engaging narrative that highlights your professional journey and sets the stage for the rest of the interview. Here are some key points to consider:

- Start with a Strong Opening Begin with a brief introduction that includes your name and your current professional role or status. This sets a clear starting point for your narrative.
- Highlight Key Career Milestones Outline the significant points in your career that have led you to where you are today.

Focus on roles, responsibilities, and achievements that are relevant to the position you are applying for.

- Emphasize Skills and Experiences Mention the skills and experiences that are most relevant to the job. This shows the interviewer that you have the background necessary to succeed in the role.
- Connect the Dots Explain how your past experiences have prepared you for this position. This helps the interviewer understand the logical progression of your career and why you are a good fit for the role.
- Keep It Concise Aim for a response that is around 1-2 minutes long. This ensures you are providing enough information without overwhelming the interviewer.

Focusing on Professional Highlights

When focusing on professional highlights, you want to ensure that you present the most impressive and relevant aspects of your career.

1. Identify Key Achievements Think about the major achievements in your career. This could be a project you led, an award you received, or a significant problem you solved. Quantify your achievements where possible. For example, "I led a marketing campaign that increased website traffic by 40% and boosted sales by 25%."

2. Showcase Your Growth Demonstrate how you have grown in your career. Highlight promotions, additional responsibilities, or skills you have acquired over time. For example, "After two years as a content writer, I was promoted to content manager, where I took on a leadership role and developed new content

strategies that enhanced our brand's online presence."

3. Relate to the Job Connect your highlights to the job you are applying for. Show the interviewer how your past successes make you a good fit for their company. For example, "My experience in developing data-driven marketing strategies aligns well with your company's focus on innovative marketing solutions."

What Are Your Strengths and Weaknesses?

Presenting Your Strengths Confidently

When asked about your strengths, you have the opportunity to showcase what you do best and how it can benefit the company.

1. Be Honest and Relevant Choose strengths that are genuinely yours and relevant to the job. For example, if you are applying for a project management role, you might say, "One

of my strengths is my ability to manage multiple projects efficiently and meet deadlines consistently."

2. Provide Examples Support your strengths with specific examples. This adds credibility to your claims. For example, "In my previous role, I managed a portfolio of five projects simultaneously, all of which were completed on time and within budget."

3. Link to the Job Explain how your strengths will help you succeed in the role you are applying for. For example, "My strong organizational skills will enable me to manage the multiple responsibilities of this role effectively, ensuring that all projects are completed to a high standard."

Discussing Weaknesses with a Positive Spin

Discussing weaknesses can be tricky, but with the right approach, you can turn this question into a positive aspect of your interview.

1. Choose a Real Weakness Select a genuine weakness, but one that is not critical to the job. For example, "I sometimes have trouble delegating tasks because I like to ensure everything is done correctly."

2. Show Self-Awareness Demonstrate that you are aware of your weakness and its impact. For example, "I realized that my reluctance to delegate could slow down the team and limit our productivity."

3. Explain Steps Taken to Improve Highlight the actions you have taken to address your weakness. This shows your commitment to personal growth. For example, "I have been working on this by learning to trust my team's

abilities and delegating more effectively. I now provide clear instructions and support, which has improved our overall efficiency."

4. End on a Positive Note Conclude by showing that your weakness has led to positive outcomes. For example, "This change has not only improved team productivity but also allowed me to focus on more strategic aspects of my role."

Why Do You Want to Work with Us?

Showing Genuine Interest in the Company

When interviewers ask why you want to work at their company, they want to see that you have done your homework and are genuinely interested in the role and the company.

1. Research the Company Learn about the company's mission, values, culture, and recent

achievements. Visit their website, read news articles, and check their social media profiles.

2. Highlight Alignment with Company Values Show how your values align with those of the company. For example, "I admire your commitment to sustainability and innovation, which are values I also hold dear."

3. Mention Specific Aspects You Admire Point out specific aspects of the company that attract you. This could be their products, services, reputation, or work environment. For example, "I am impressed by your company's innovative approach to technology and how you have consistently been a leader in the industry."

Connecting Your Goals with the Company's Vision

1. Align Your Career Goals Explain how the role aligns with your long-term career goals. For example, "I am looking to develop my skills in

product management, and your company's focus on cutting-edge technology provides the perfect environment for my growth."

2. Show How You Can Contribute Highlight how your skills and experiences can contribute to the company's success. For example, "With my background in digital marketing and project management, I believe I can contribute significantly to your upcoming product launches and marketing campaigns."

3. Express Enthusiasm Show your enthusiasm for the role and the company. Genuine enthusiasm can set you apart from other candidates. For example, "I am excited about the possibility of working with such a talented team and contributing to projects that make a real difference."

Chapter 4: Behavioral Interview Questions

Behavioral interview questions are designed to assess how candidates have behaved in past situations as a predictor of future performance. These questions often delve into specific examples from your professional history to gauge your skills, abilities, and fit for the role. To effectively respond to these questions, candidates often use the STAR method.

STAR Method: Situation, Task, Action, Result
The STAR method is a structured approach used to answer behavioral interview questions. It stands for Situation, Task, Action, and Result. Here's how each component contributes to a comprehensive answer:

What the STAR Framework is All About

Situation: Begin by providing context for the interviewer. Describe the situation you were in or the challenge you faced. Be concise and focus on the key details relevant to the question.

Task: Explain what your role and responsibilities were in that situation. Clarify the specific task or objective you needed to accomplish.

Action: Detail the actions you took to address the situation or task. This is the most critical part where you demonstrate your skills and decision-making process. Highlight what steps you took, why you chose them, and how you implemented them.

Result: Conclude by outlining the outcomes of your actions. What was achieved as a result of your efforts? Quantify the results if possible (e.g., increased sales by 20%, reduced processing time by 30%, etc.). Focus on the positive impact and what you learned from the experience.

Applying the STAR Method to Your Answers

- Practice using the STAR method with various examples from your work experience. Choose examples that highlight relevant skills and achievements related to the job you are applying for.
- Structure your answers logically, starting with the Situation and Task, moving into the Action you took, and concluding with the Result. This structured approach helps you stay focused and ensures you cover all necessary aspects of your story.
- Tailor each answer to the specific question asked. Be prepared to adapt your examples to different types of

behavioral questions (e.g., problem-solving, teamwork, leadership).

Tell Me About a Time You Faced a Challenge

This question aims to assess your problem-solving abilities and how you handle adversity in the workplace. When responding:

Selecting Relevant Examples

- Choose an example where you encountered a significant challenge relevant to the job you are applying for. This could involve overcoming obstacles, resolving conflicts, or meeting tight deadlines.
- Ensure the challenge was substantial enough to demonstrate your skills and perseverance. Avoid trivial examples that may not showcase your abilities effectively.

Highlighting Your Problem-Solving Skills

- Use the STAR method to structure your response. Describe the challenge (Situation), what needed to be done (Task), the steps you took (Action), and the positive outcomes (Result).
- Emphasize your problem-solving approach and decision-making process. Discuss why you chose certain actions and how you evaluated alternatives.
- Reflect on what you learned from overcoming the challenge and how it has contributed to your professional growth.

Describe a Successful Project You Managed
Employers often ask about projects you've managed to gauge your leadership, organizational skills, and ability to deliver results.

When answering:

Detailing Your Role and Contributions:

- Clearly define the project scope, objectives, and your specific role in managing it. Describe the project's timeline, budget, and any challenges you faced.
- Use the STAR method to structure your response. Explain the Situation and Task, outline the Actions you took to manage the project effectively, and discuss the positive Results achieved.
- Highlight key milestones, achievements, and how you kept the project on track. Demonstrate your ability to prioritize tasks, allocate resources, and mitigate risks.

Demonstrating Leadership and Teamwork

- Showcase your leadership skills by discussing how you motivated and guided your team. Describe any decisions you made that influenced the project's success.
- Discuss how you collaborated with team members, stakeholders, and other departments. Highlight instances where you resolved conflicts or facilitated communication.
- Share insights into what you learned from managing the project and how it has prepared you for similar challenges in the future.

Chapter 5: Technical and Job-Specific Questions

Preparing for Technical Questions
Reviewing Key Concepts and Practices

When you're preparing for technical questions, it's important to go over the fundamental ideas and methods that are essential to your field of work or study. This means going back to basics and revisiting the core principles that underpin your daily work. I mean revisiting the basic principles and procedures that professionals in your industry use every day. For example, if you're in software development, you might review programming languages, algorithms, and design patterns.

Reviewing key concepts ensures that you have a solid foundation to build upon when facing technical questions. It helps you recall important information quickly and apply it effectively in problem-solving situations.

Practicing Problem-Solving Scenarios

In technical interviews or assessments, you're often asked to solve problems or explain how you would approach certain challenges. Practicing these scenarios involves doing mock exercises where you tackle these types of problems. For software engineers, this could mean writing code to solve algorithmic challenges or designing a system architecture to meet certain requirements or troubleshooting issues based on real-world scenarios.

Regular practice not only sharpens your problem-solving skills but also boosts your confidence in applying theoretical knowledge to practical situations. It helps you identify areas where you need more practice or further understanding, ensuring that you're well-prepared for any technical assessment.

Demonstrating Your Industry Knowledge
Staying Updated with Industry Trends

Industries are dynamic, constantly evolving with new technologies, methodologies, and trends. To demonstrate your industry knowledge effectively, you need to stay informed about these changes. This involves actively seeking out information through various channels such as industry publications, blogs, podcasts, and professional networks.

For example, if you're in artificial intelligence, staying updated might mean following the latest research breakthroughs, understanding the ethical implications of AI technologies, and learning about new tools and frameworks being developed. This proactive approach not only keeps you abreast of current developments but also positions you as a forward-thinking professional who can anticipate and adapt to industry changes.

Sharing Insights and Expertise

Demonstrating your industry knowledge goes beyond personal awareness; it also involves sharing your insights and expertise with others. This could take various forms, such as writing articles or blog posts, giving presentations at conferences or meet-ups, mentoring junior colleagues, or participating in online forums and discussions.

When you share your knowledge, you not only contribute to the collective learning of your profession but also enhance your own understanding through teaching and dialogue. It showcases your communication skills, leadership potential, and commitment to advancing your field. Moreover, sharing insights can lead to valuable connections and opportunities for collaboration or career advancement.

Chapter 6: Questions to Ask the Interviewer

When you're interviewing for a job, it's important not only to answer the interviewer's questions but also to ask your own. Asking thoughtful questions can leave a lasting impression, show your interest in the role and the company, and help you evaluate whether the company culture aligns with your values and career goals. This chapter will guide you through how to prepare these questions and what to consider when evaluating the company's culture.

Making a Lasting Impression
Preparing Thoughtful Questions

Asking thoughtful questions during an interview shows that you are genuinely interested in the role and the company. It indicates that you have done your homework and are looking for a long-term fit. Here's how you can prepare these questions:

1. Research the Company: Start by researching the company thoroughly. Look at their website, recent news articles, and any available annual reports. Understand their products, services, mission, values, and recent developments. This background knowledge will help you formulate relevant questions.

2. Know the Role: Review the job description carefully. Understand the responsibilities and qualifications required. Think about how your skills and experiences align with the role and what you might need to know more about to succeed in it

3. Reflect on Your Career Goals: Consider your own career aspirations. What do you hope to achieve in this role? What skills do you want to

develop? Prepare questions that help you understand if this job aligns with your goals.

4. Tailor Your Questions: Based on your research and reflection, prepare a list of questions that are specific to the company and the role. Avoid generic questions that you could easily find the answers to online. Instead, focus on questions that show your interest and curiosity about the specifics of the job and the company.

Typical examples of Thoughtful Questions are given below:

A. About the Role:

1. "Can you describe a typical day for someone in this position?"
2. "What are the most immediate challenges facing the team, and how can I help address them?"

3. "What are the key performance indicators (KPIs) for this role?"

B. About the Team and Management:

1. "Can you tell me more about the team I will be working with?"
2. "What is your management style, and how do you support your team's development?"

C. About the Company:

1. "How does the company measure success in this department?"
2. "What are the company's goals for the next five years, and how does this role contribute to those goals?"

D. About Professional Development:

1. "What opportunities for growth and development are available?"

2. "Are there any training programs or professional development initiatives?"

Showing Interest in the Role and Company

Showing genuine interest in the role and the company can set you apart from other candidates. Here are some tips on how to convey your enthusiasm effectively:

1. Be Specific: When discussing why you are interested in the role, be specific about what aspects of the job excite you. Relate these to your past experiences and career aspirations.

2. Connect with Company Values: If you find that the company's values align with your own, mention this in the interview. Explain why these values are important to you and how they influence your work.

3. Discuss Recent Developments: Bring up recent news about the company, such as new projects, partnerships, or achievements. This

shows that you are up-to-date and keen on the company's activities.

4. **Engage Actively:** During the interview, listen carefully and engage actively with what the interviewer is saying. Ask follow-up questions based on their responses to show that you are paying attention and are genuinely curious.

5. **Share Your Vision:** If appropriate, share your vision for your potential future at the company. Talk about how you see yourself contributing to the team and the company's success.

You can demonstrate showing interest by adopting any of the following examples:

- "I was excited to read about your recent expansion into new markets. How do you see this impacting the team and this role specifically?"

- "I appreciate the company's commitment to sustainability. Can you tell me more about how this role can contribute to these initiatives?"
- "Your focus on innovation is something I value greatly. I would love to hear more about the company's current projects in this area."

Evaluating the Company Culture
Understanding the company culture is crucial to determine if you will be happy and productive in the new role. Here's how you can assess the culture during your interview process:

Understanding Team Dynamics

Team dynamics can significantly affect your work experience and job satisfaction. Here are some aspects to consider and questions to ask:

- Team Structure: Understand how the team is structured. Are there clear roles and responsibilities? How does the team collaborate?

- Communication Style: Ask about the team's communication style. Is it formal or informal? How are decisions made and communicated?
- Conflict Resolution: Find out how the team handles conflicts. A healthy approach to conflict resolution can indicate a supportive and respectful work environment.
- Team Interactions: Observe and ask about how team members interact with each other. Are there opportunities for team bonding and social interactions?
- Diversity and Inclusion: Ask about the company's commitment to diversity and inclusion. A diverse team can bring in a variety of perspectives and ideas.

Questions to Understand Team Dynamics:

- ✓ Can you describe the team I will be working with and how it is structured?
- ✓ How does the team typically communicate and collaborate on projects?"
- ✓ Can you give me an example of how the team handled a recent challenge or conflict?"
- ✓ What opportunities are there for team members to interact and bond outside of work-related tasks?"
- ✓ How does the company support diversity and inclusion within teams?"

Assessing Growth and Development Opportunities

Knowing that a company supports your growth and development can make a significant difference in your career satisfaction and progression. Here's how to evaluate these opportunities:

- Training Programs: Ask about any formal training programs that the company offers. These could be related to your specific role or general professional skills.
- Career Advancement: Find out about the typical career path for someone in your position. Are there opportunities for promotion and advancement?
- Mentorship and Support: Ask if the company offers mentorship programs. Having a mentor can be invaluable for your personal and professional growth.
- Performance Reviews: Inquire about the performance review process. How often are reviews conducted, and what criteria are used to evaluate performance?
- Skill Development: Understand how the company supports ongoing skill development. Are there opportunities to

attend workshops, conferences, or further education?

Questions to Assess Growth and Development:

- What kind of training programs does the company offer to employees?"
- "Can you describe the typical career path for someone in this role?"
- "Does the company have a mentorship program, and how does it work?"
- "How are performance reviews conducted, and what criteria are used?"
- "What opportunities are there for continuous learning and skill development?"

Chapter 7: Handling Difficult Questions

In this chapter, we'll explore how to handle some difficult questions most related to employment gaps in your work history and salary expectations.

Addressing Employment Gaps

There might be periods where you weren't employed. This could be due to various reasons such as taking a break to pursue further education, dealing with personal matters, or facing challenges in finding a new job. While these gaps can seem like red flags to potential employers, there are strategies you can use to address them positively and honestly. Let's delve into two key approaches: being honest and positive, and turning gaps into strengths.

Being Honest and Positive

When faced with questions about employment gaps during a job interview, honesty is crucial. It's essential to acknowledge the gap in your employment history and provide a brief explanation without going into unnecessary detail. Being upfront about the reasons for the gap demonstrates integrity and transparency to the interviewer. Here are some tips for handling employment gaps with honesty and positivity:

1. Acknowledge the Gap: Start by acknowledging the gap in your employment history when asked about it during the interview. You can say something like, "Yes, there was a gap in my employment from [start date] to [end date]."

2. Provide a Brief Explanation: Offer a concise explanation for the gap without dwelling on negative aspects. Focus on the reasons that led to the gap, such as personal development, family responsibilities, or career exploration.

3. Highlight Positive Activities: Emphasize any productive activities you engaged in during the gap period. This could include volunteer work, freelance projects, skill-building courses, or

traveling experiences. Highlighting these activities demonstrates your proactive approach to self-improvement and professional development.

4. Showcase Transferable Skills: Discuss how the experiences gained during the gap period have equipped you with valuable skills that are relevant to the job you're applying for. Whether it's communication, problem-solving, or time management skills, illustrate how these abilities can benefit the prospective employer.

5. Stay Positive: Maintain a positive attitude throughout the conversation. Avoid speaking negatively about past employers or dwelling on the challenges you faced during the gap. Instead, focus on the lessons learned and how you've grown from the experience.

Turning Gaps into Amazing Strengths

While employment gaps may initially seem like setbacks, they can also present opportunities for personal and professional growth. By reframing these gaps as strengths, you can position yourself as a resilient and adaptable candidate to potential employers. Here are some strategies for turning employment gaps into strengths:

1. Showcase Learning and Development: Highlight any learning experiences or professional development initiatives you pursued during the gap period. This could include enrolling in online courses, attending workshops or conferences, or acquiring certifications relevant to your field. By demonstrating your commitment to continuous learning, you showcase your dedication to self-improvement.

2. Emphasize Problem-Solving Skills: Reflect on any challenges you faced during the gap and describe how you successfully navigated them. Employers value candidates who can demonstrate resilience, adaptability, and problem-solving abilities. Use specific examples to illustrate how

you overcame obstacles and emerged stronger as a result.

3. Highlight Volunteer Work and Community Involvement: If you were involved in volunteer work or community initiatives during the gap period, make sure to highlight these experiences. Volunteer work demonstrates your commitment to making a positive impact beyond the workplace and showcases your ability to contribute to the community.

4. Discuss Freelance or Contract Projects: If you took on freelance or contract projects during the gap, discuss the skills you acquired and the results you achieved. Whether it was designing websites, writing articles, or providing consulting services, freelance work demonstrates your ability to work independently, manage projects, and deliver results.

5. Connect the Gap to the Job: Finally, bridge the gap between your past experiences and the job

you're applying for. Explain how the skills and experiences gained during the gap period align with the requirements of the position and make you a strong fit for the role

Discussing Salary Expectations
Talking about salary can be uncomfortable, but it's an essential part of the job search process. Here are some tips for handling this conversation:

Researching Market Rates

Before going into an interview, research the average salary for the position you're applying for. You can use online resources, salary surveys, or ask people in your industry. Knowing the market rate will give you a good idea of what to expect and help you negotiate more confidently.

Negotiating Confidently

When discussing salary, be confident in what you're asking for. Start by stating your desired salary range based on your research. Be prepared to justify why you think you're worth that amount. Talk about your skills, experience, and the value you'll bring to the company. It's okay to negotiate, but be respectful and professional throughout the process.

Chapter 8: Follow-Up and Next Steps

Post-Interview Etiquette

After you've had an interview, there are several important steps to follow to leave a positive impression and maintain professionalism.

Sending Thank You Notes

Sending a thank you note after an interview is a crucial step that shows appreciation and reinforces your interest in the position. Here's how to do it effectively:

- Timing Send your thank you note within 24-48 hours after the interview. This shows promptness and enthusiasm.
- Personalization Address each interviewer individually if possible. Mention specific points discussed during the interview to personalize your message.

- Content Express gratitude for the opportunity to interview. Reiterate your interest in the position and highlight a key strength or two that align with what was discussed.
- Format Email is generally the preferred method today, as it's quick and ensures timely delivery. However, handwritten notes can be appropriate for certain industries or positions.

Following Up Professionally

After sending your thank you note, you may need to follow up if you haven't heard back within the expected timeframe. Here are tips on how to do it professionally:

- Timing Wait at least a week after the thank you note before following up. This gives the hiring manager or recruiter sufficient time to make decisions.

- Method Email is generally the preferred method for follow-ups as well. Keep your email brief, polite, and to the point.
- Content Inquire about the status of your application. Reaffirm your interest in the position and express your enthusiasm about the opportunity to contribute to the team.
- Patience Be patient and respectful in your follow-up. Hiring processes can take time, and it's important not to come across as pushy or impatient.

Handling Rejections and Offers
Dealing with both rejections and offers is a natural part of the job search process. Here's how to navigate these situations effectively:

Learning from Rejections

Receiving a rejection can be disappointing, but it's important to approach it as a learning experience:

- Mindset Stay positive and view rejection as an opportunity to grow and improve.
- Feedback If possible, ask for feedback from the interviewer to understand why you weren't selected. Use this feedback constructively to identify areas for improvement.
- Self-reflection Reflect on your performance during the interview. Consider what went well and what you could do differently in future interviews.
- Persistence Don't let rejection discourage you. Keep applying for other opportunities and continue refining your skills and interview techniques.

Evaluating Job Offers

When you receive a job offer, it's important to carefully evaluate it to ensure it aligns with your career goals and expectations:

- Compensation Consider the salary, benefits, and any perks offered. Evaluate whether they meet your financial needs and expectations.
- Job Responsibilities Review the job description and responsibilities. Ensure they align with your skills, interests, and career aspirations.
- Company Culture Assess the company culture and work environment. Consider whether you would fit in well with the team and enjoy working there.

- Opportunities for Growth Evaluate potential opportunities for career growth and development within the company.
- Decision Making Take your time to consider the offer. Avoid making hasty decisions. It's okay to ask for some time to think it over before providing a response.
- Negotiation If aspects of the offer don't meet your expectations, consider negotiating. Be prepared to discuss your reasons for negotiating and approach it professionally.

Chapter 9: Special Situations

Group Interviews and Assessment Centers

Group interviews and assessment centers are methods used by organizations to evaluate multiple candidates simultaneously. They are designed to assess various skills and qualities that are important for the role being applied for. Here's a detailed look at what each bullet point entails:

Preparing for Group Dynamics

In a group interview or assessment center, candidates interact with each other while participating in tasks or discussions. Preparation involves understanding how to navigate group dynamics effectively. This includes:

- Understanding Roles: Knowing your role within the group and how to contribute positively.

- Active Listening: Paying attention to others' ideas and viewpoints.
- Conflict Resolution: Being able to handle disagreements constructively.
- Leadership and Followership: Knowing when to take a lead and when to support others' leadership.

Excelling in Collaborative Tasks

Candidates often engage in collaborative tasks to demonstrate teamwork and problem-solving skills. Excelling in these tasks involves:

- Contributing Ideas: Sharing relevant ideas and solutions.
- Team Communication: Effectively expressing thoughts and listening to others.
- Flexibility: Being adaptable to changes within the group's dynamics or task requirements.

- Decision Making: Participating in group decisions and supporting the consensus.

Remote and Virtual Interviews

With the rise of technology, remote and virtual interviews have become common. These interviews are conducted online, typically via video conferencing tools. Here's what you need to know to navigate them successfully:

Mastering Video Interviewing Techniques

Video interviews require specific techniques to ensure effective communication and presentation:

- Technical Setup: Familiarize yourself with the video conferencing platform being used.
- Camera Presence: Maintain eye contact with the camera to simulate direct eye contact with the interviewer.

- Body Language: Sit upright and use gestures appropriately to convey engagement and interest.
- Clear Communication: Speak clearly and at a moderate pace to ensure your message is understood.
- Dress Professionally: Dress as you would for an in-person interview to convey professionalism.

Ensuring a Professional Setup

Creating a conducive environment is crucial for a successful virtual interview:

- ✓ Location: Choose a quiet, well-lit space with minimal distractions.
- ✓ Background: Ensure a neutral and tidy background to avoid distractions.
- ✓ Internet Connection: Use a stable internet connection to prevent disruptions.

✓ Equipment Check: Test your microphone, camera, and lighting before the interview to avoid technical issues.

Chapter 10: Continuing Your Career Growth

In the journey of career development, securing a job is only the beginning. To truly thrive in your professional life, it's essential to focus on continuous career growth. This chapter will guide you through strategies and practices that will help you maintain momentum, adapt to changing environments, and achieve long-term success.

Building Professional Growth

A. Networking Effectively

Networking is like making friends, but for your career. When you network, you meet and connect with people who can help you with your job or career goals. It's not just about meeting lots of people; it's about building relationships based on mutual interests and goals. Here's how you can network effectively:

1. Know Your Goals: Before you start networking, think about what you want to achieve. Do you want to find a new job? Learn more about a specific industry? Knowing your goals will help you focus your networking efforts.

2. Be Genuine: People can tell when you're being fake. Instead of trying to impress everyone you meet, focus on being genuine and building real connections.

3. Listen More Than You Talk: Networking is not just about talking about yourself. It's also about listening to others and learning from them. Ask questions and show genuine interest in what others have to say.

4. Follow Up: After you meet someone, don't forget to follow up. Send them an email or connect with them on LinkedIn to keep the conversation going.

5. Give Back: Networking is a two-way street. If someone helps you, try to help them in return. It

could be as simple as offering advice or making an introduction.

B. Maintaining Connections:

Once you've made connections, it's important to maintain them. Here's how you can do that:

1. Stay in Touch: Don't let your connections fade away. Make an effort to stay in touch with them regularly. It could be as simple as sending them a quick email or meeting up for coffee.

2. Offer Help: If you see an opportunity to help one of your connections, don't hesitate to offer your assistance. It could be something small like sharing an article or something bigger like making an introduction.

3. Be Reliable: When you make promises to your connections, make sure you follow through.

Being reliable will help you build trust and strengthen your relationships.

4. Celebrate Their Successes: When one of your connections achieves something, celebrate with them. It will show that you care about their success and strengthen your bond.

Lifelong Learning and Development
Embracing Continuous Education

In today's fast-paced world, learning doesn't stop once you finish school. It's important to embrace continuous education throughout your career. Here's why:

1. Stay Relevant: Industries are constantly evolving, and new technologies and techniques are always emerging. By continuing to learn, you can stay up-to-date with the latest trends and remain relevant in your field.

2. Expand Your Skills: Continuous education allows you to expand your skills and knowledge beyond your current role. This can open up new

opportunities for career advancement and personal growth.

3. Adapt to Change: The world is constantly changing, and the skills that are in demand today may not be in demand tomorrow. By continuously learning, you can adapt to these changes and future-proof your career.

4. Personal Fulfillment: Learning is not just about advancing your career; it's also about personal fulfillment. Whether you're learning a new language, mastering a new hobby, or studying a new subject, continuous education can enrich your life in many ways.

Setting Career Goals

Setting career goals is like planning a road trip. It gives you direction and helps you stay focused on where you want to go. Here's how you can set effective career goals:

1. Be Specific: Instead of setting vague goals like "get a promotion," be specific about what you want to achieve and when you want to achieve it. For example, "get promoted to manager within the next two years."

2. Make Them Attainable: While it's good to aim high, make sure your goals are attainable. Setting unrealistic goals can lead to frustration and disappointment.

3. Set Deadlines: Deadlines can help you stay motivated and accountable. When setting goals, give yourself a deadline to work towards.

4. Break Them Down: Big goals can seem overwhelming, so break them down into smaller, more manageable tasks. This will make them less intimidating and easier to tackle.

5. Review and Adjust: Your career goals may change over time, and that's okay. Periodically review your goals and adjust them as needed to reflect your evolving priorities and aspirations.

By building professional relationships, embracing continuous education, and setting career goals, you can continue to grow and thrive in your career. These are lifelong practices that will serve you well no matter where your career takes you.

Your Path to Success
Developing Soft Skills

While technical skills are crucial, soft skills like communication, leadership, and emotional intelligence are equally important. They enhance your ability to work effectively with others and navigate complex professional environments. Here are some of the soft skills to develop.

- **Communication Skills**: Practice active listening, clear articulation of ideas, and constructive feedback. Engaging in public speaking or presentation opportunities can also help.
- **Leadership and Teamwork**: Volunteer for leadership roles in projects or

organizations. Learn to delegate, motivate, and manage conflicts effectively.

- **Emotional Intelligence:** Develop self-awareness, empathy, and the ability to manage your emotions and relationships constructively. Mindfulness and reflective practices can enhance these skills.

Summarizing Key Takeaways

Success can mean different things to different people, but in general, it often involves achieving goals that are important to you. To reach your version of success, it's essential to understand what steps can help you get there. Here are some key takeaways:

- Setting Clear Goals: Begin by defining what success means to you. Is it about your career, personal life, relationships, or something else? Setting clear, specific goals gives you something concrete to work towards.

- Planning and Strategy: Once you have your goals in mind, develop a plan to achieve them. Break down your goals into smaller, manageable steps. This helps to create a roadmap that guides you through your journey to success.
- Continuous Learning: Success often requires acquiring new knowledge and skills. Stay curious and open to learning. This might involve formal education, self-study, or learning from experiences and mistakes.
- Adaptability: Life can be unpredictable, and setbacks are a part of any journey. Being adaptable means being able to adjust your plans and strategies when faced with challenges or unexpected changes.

- Persistence: Success rarely happens overnight. It often requires hard work, determination, and resilience. Stay committed to your goals even when faced with obstacles or temporary failures.
- Seeking Support: Success is seldom achieved alone. Surround yourself with supportive people who encourage and believe in you. Seek mentors or role models who can provide guidance and advice based on their own experiences.
- Celebrating Milestones: Acknowledge and celebrate your achievements along the way. This boosts your confidence and motivation, reinforcing your commitment to your path to success.

2. Encouraging Confidence and Persistence

Confidence and persistence are crucial elements on the path to success. Here's a deeper look into what each of these entails:

- Confidence: Believe in yourself and your abilities. Confidence is about trusting that you have the skills and qualities needed to achieve your goals. It involves having a positive mindset and overcoming self-doubt.

    ✓ Building Confidence: Start by recognizing your strengths and talents. Set achievable goals and celebrate small victories. Practice positive self-talk and challenge negative thoughts that undermine your confidence.

    ✓ Facing Challenges: Confidence helps you tackle challenges with a proactive attitude. Instead of being paralyzed by fear of failure, confident individuals see setbacks as opportunities for growth and learning.

✓ Seeking Feedback: Actively seek constructive feedback from others. This helps you identify areas for improvement and build on your strengths. Accept feedback gracefully and use it to refine your skills and approaches.

- Persistence: Persistence is the determination to continue striving towards your goals despite obstacles or difficulties. It involves staying committed to your vision and taking consistent action.

  ✓ Developing Persistence: Cultivate a mindset of perseverance. Understand that setbacks and failures are natural parts of any journey. Learn from setbacks, adjust your strategies if needed, and keep moving forward.

✓ Managing Setbacks: When faced with challenges, persistence helps you maintain focus and motivation. Break down challenges into smaller tasks, seek advice or support if necessary, and keep working towards your goals.

✓ Staying Motivated: Persistence is fueled by your passion and dedication to your goals. Remind yourself why you started and visualize the outcome you want to achieve. Stay inspired by surrounding yourself with positive influences and role models.

Sample Interview Questions and Answers

To wrap up and guide you toward achieving your dream job after covering the fundamentals of job interview preparation, here are 20 frequently asked interview questions alongside expert answers.

List of 20 Common Questions

1. Tell me about yourself.

2. Why do you want to work here?

3. What are your strengths?

4. What are your weaknesses?

5. Why are you leaving your current job?

6. Where do you see yourself in five years?

7. Can you describe a challenging situation and how you handled it?

8. What are your salary expectations?

9. Why should we hire you?

10. Tell me about a time you demonstrated leadership skills.

11. How do you handle stress and pressure?

12. What do you know about our company?

13. Tell me about a time you made a mistake. How did you handle it?

14. How do you prioritize your work?

15. What is your greatest professional achievement?

16. Describe a time when you had to work as part of a team.

17. How do you handle feedback and criticism?

18. Tell me about a time you had a conflict with a coworker and how you resolved it.

19. What motivates you?

20. Do you have any questions for us

Model Answers From Professionals

Responses from a Software Developer

These answers are tailored to highlight your skills and experiences as a software developer, showcasing your technical expertise and ability to work effectively within a team.

1. Tell me about yourself.

"I have over six years of experience in software development, with a strong focus on web applications and backend systems. I hold a degree in Computer Science from Stanford University. Throughout my career, I've worked with various programming languages, including Java, Python, and JavaScript. At my last job, I led a project to migrate a legacy system to a modern micro services architecture, which improved system performance by 40%."

2. Why do you want to work here?

"I'm impressed by your company's innovative approach to technology and your commitment to creating cutting-edge software solutions. I'm particularly excited about the opportunity to work on your Money-Gate App because I have a strong background in Frontend and Backend technologies, and I believe I can contribute significantly to your team's success."

3. What are your strengths?

"One of my key strengths is my ability to quickly learn and adapt to new technologies. I am also skilled at problem-solving and debugging complex issues, which allows me to ensure the stability and performance of the software. Additionally, my strong collaboration skills help me work effectively with cross-functional teams."

4. What are your weaknesses?

"I sometimes get deeply involved in debugging and optimizing code, which can lead to spending more time than necessary on certain tasks.

However, I've been working on improving this by setting time limits for debugging sessions and asking for help when needed to ensure timely completion of projects."

5. Why are you leaving your current job?

"I've gained valuable experience at my current job, but I'm looking for new challenges that align more closely with my career goals. I'm particularly interested in working at your company because of its reputation for technological innovation and the opportunity to work on large-scale projects."

6. Where do you see yourself in five years?

"In five years, I see myself taking on more leadership responsibilities within the software development team, possibly as a senior developer or team lead. I aim to contribute to major projects and mentor junior developers, helping the team achieve its goals and advancing the company's technological capabilities."

7. Can you describe a challenging situation and how you handled it?

"In a recent project, we encountered significant performance issues with our database queries, which were impacting user experience. I led a team to diagnose the problem, identified inefficient queries, and optimized them. Additionally, we implemented caching strategies, which reduced load times by 50% and improved overall system performance."

8. What are your salary expectations?

"Based on my research and experience, I am expecting a salary in the range of $100,000 to $150,000. However, I am open to discussing this further and am flexible based on the overall compensation package and growth opportunities."

9. Why should we hire you?

"I bring a strong technical background and a proven track record of successfully completing complex projects. My expertise in [specific technology] and my ability to collaborate effectively with team members make me a strong candidate for this role. I'm confident that my skills and experience will enable me to contribute positively to your team."

10. Tell me about a time you demonstrated leadership skills.

"At my previous job, I led a team of developers on a critical project to develop a new feature for our application. I organized regular meetings to track progress, assigned tasks based on each member's strengths, and provided guidance and support. The project was completed ahead of schedule and received positive feedback from both the client and end-users."

11. How do you handle stress and pressure?

"I handle stress by staying organized and breaking down tasks into manageable steps. I prioritize my work to ensure that critical tasks are completed first. Additionally, I find that taking short breaks to clear my mind helps me stay focused and maintain productivity under pressure."

12. What do you know about our company?

"Your company is a leader in [industry], known for its innovative software solutions and commitment to quality. I've been following your recent projects, such as [specific project], and I'm impressed by the impact they've had on the market. Your emphasis on continuous improvement and cutting-edge technology aligns well with my career goals."

13. Tell me about a time you made a mistake. How did you handle it?

"I once introduced a bug into our codebase that caused a significant issue in production. As soon as I realized the mistake, I immediately informed my team and we worked together to identify the root cause and deploy a fix. I also conducted a thorough post-mortem analysis to understand how the mistake happened and implemented additional code reviews to prevent similar issues in the future."

14. How do you prioritize your work?

"I prioritize my work by assessing the urgency and importance of each task. I use project management tools to keep track of deadlines and milestones, and I regularly review my priorities to ensure alignment with project goals. I also communicate with my team to stay updated on any changes and adjust my priorities accordingly."

15. What is your greatest professional achievement?

"My greatest professional achievement was leading a project to migrate our application to a cloud-based infrastructure. This involved extensive planning, coordination with different teams, and overcoming several technical challenges. The migration was completed successfully, resulting in improved scalability, performance, and cost efficiency."

16. Describe a time when you had to work as part of a team.

"During a major product release, I worked closely with a team of developers, QA engineers, and product managers. We held regular meetings to discuss progress, address issues, and ensure alignment. By collaborating effectively, we were able to meet our deadlines and deliver a high-quality product that met all requirements and exceeded user expectations."

17. How do you handle feedback and criticism?

"I view feedback and criticism as valuable opportunities for growth. I listen carefully, ask clarifying questions if needed, and reflect on how I can improve. For example, after receiving feedback on my code documentation, I made it a priority to enhance the clarity and thoroughness of my comments, which helped improve team collaboration and understanding."

18. Tell me about a time you had a conflict with a coworker and how you resolved it.

"I once had a disagreement with a coworker about the design approach for a new feature. I suggested we sit down and discuss our perspectives in detail. By listening to each other and considering the pros and cons of each approach, we were able to reach a consensus and implement a solution that satisfied both of us and met the project's requirements."

19. What motivates you?

"I am motivated by the opportunity to solve complex problems and create software that makes a difference. Seeing my code in action and knowing that it positively impacts users is incredibly rewarding. Additionally, I enjoy learning new technologies and continuously improving my skills to stay current in the rapidly evolving field of software development."

20. Do you have any questions for us?

"Yes, I do. Can you tell me more about the team I would be working with? What are the main challenges you expect the team to face in the coming year? How do you support professional development and growth within the company? Additionally, I'm interested in learning more about your development process and the technologies you use."

Responses from a Customer Representive Role
1. Tell me about yourself.

"I have over five years of experience in customer service, with a focus on resolving issues efficiently and maintaining high levels of customer satisfaction. I hold a degree in Communications, and I thrive in fast-paced environments where I can use my problem-solving skills to help customers. My goal is always to provide a positive and seamless experience for customers."

2. Why do you want to work here?

"I am impressed by your company's commitment to customer satisfaction and your reputation for innovation in the industry. I am particularly drawn to your emphasis on professional development and team collaboration. I believe my skills and passion for helping customers align well with your company's values and goals."

3. What are your strengths?

"My strengths include excellent communication skills, a strong ability to empathize with customers, and effective problem-solving abilities. I am adept at handling high-stress situations and can quickly adapt to changing circumstances. My attention to detail ensures that I can provide accurate information and solutions to customers."

4. What are your weaknesses?

"I can sometimes be overly focused on ensuring that each customer interaction is perfect, which can slow me down. However, I am working on balancing thoroughness with efficiency to ensure that I meet performance metrics without compromising the quality of service."

5. Why are you leaving your current job?

- "I have learned a great deal in my current role, but I am looking for new challenges and opportunities for growth. I am particularly interested in your company because of its strong reputation in the industry and the potential to develop my skills further while contributing to a dynamic team."

6. Where do you see yourself in five years?

"In five years, I see myself in a leadership role within customer service, perhaps as a team lead or manager. I aim to continue developing my skills, contribute to the success of the company, and help train and mentor new team members to provide excellent customer service."

7. Can you describe a challenging situation and how you handled it?

"Once, I dealt with a customer who was very upset about a billing error. I listened to their concerns without interrupting, apologized for the inconvenience, and assured them that I would resolve the issue. I quickly reviewed their account, identified the mistake, and corrected it. I also followed up with them later to ensure they were satisfied with the resolution. This approach not only resolved the issue but also turned a frustrated customer into a loyal one."

8. What are your salary expectations?

"Based on my research and experience, I am expecting a salary in the range of $50,000 to $100,000. However, I am open to discussing this further and am flexible based on the overall compensation package, benefits, and opportunities for growth."

9. Why should we hire you?

"I bring a strong background in customer service, excellent communication skills, and a proven ability to resolve issues efficiently. My dedication to customer satisfaction and my ability to remain calm under pressure will make me a valuable asset to your team. I am confident that my experience and passion for helping customers will contribute positively to your company."

10. Tell me about a time you demonstrated leadership skills.

"In my previous role, I often took the initiative to mentor new team members. For example, I created a training manual to help them understand our processes and systems more quickly. I also led team meetings to share best practices and provide support during busy periods. My efforts helped improve team performance and fostered a collaborative environment."

11. How do you handle stress and pressure?

"I handle stress by staying organized and prioritizing my tasks. I break down large tasks into smaller, manageable steps and set realistic deadlines. I also practice mindfulness and take short breaks to stay focused and calm. These strategies help me maintain high performance even in high-pressure situations."

12. What do you know about our company?

"Your company is known for its exceptional customer service and innovative solutions in Telecommunication. I am impressed by your commitment to continuous improvement and the way you prioritize customer satisfaction. Your recent initiatives in customer center technology demonstrate your leadership in the industry and your focus on meeting customer needs."

13. Tell me about a time you made a mistake. How did you handle it?

"I once mistakenly provided incorrect information to a customer regarding a product return policy. As soon as I realized the mistake, I contacted the customer to apologize and provide the correct information. I also offered a small discount on their next purchase as a gesture of goodwill. This experience taught me the importance of double-checking information and being proactive in correcting errors."

14. How do you prioritize your work?

"I prioritize my work by assessing the urgency and importance of each task. I use a task management system to keep track of customer inquiries and follow-ups. I ensure that urgent issues are addressed first while also managing ongoing tasks efficiently. Effective time management and clear communication with customers and colleagues are key to my process."

15. What is your greatest professional achievement?

"My greatest professional achievement was implementing a new customer feedback system that increased our customer satisfaction scores by 20%. By analyzing feedback and identifying common issues, I was able to propose and implement changes that improved our service delivery and customer experience significantly."

16. Describe a time when you had to work as part of a team.

"In a project to improve our customer service response time, I worked closely with my team to analyze our current processes and identify bottlenecks. We collaborated to develop new protocols and training programs. By leveraging each team member's strengths, we successfully reduced our average response time by 30%, which greatly enhanced our customer satisfaction."

17. How do you handle feedback and criticism?

"I view feedback and criticism as valuable opportunities for growth. I listen carefully, ask clarifying questions if needed, and reflect on how I can improve. For example, after receiving feedback on my call handling skills, I attended a workshop and practiced new techniques, which improved my ability to resolve customer issues more efficiently and effectively."

18. Tell me about a time you had a conflict with a coworker and how you resolved it.

"I had a disagreement with a coworker about the best approach to handle a customer complaint. I suggested we discuss our perspectives and find a compromise. Through open communication and focusing on our common goal of providing excellent customer service, we reached a solution that satisfied both of us and improved our teamwork."

19. What motivates you?

"I am motivated by the opportunity to help customers and make a positive impact on their experience with the company. Solving problems and ensuring customer satisfaction is incredibly rewarding. Continuous learning and professional development also keep me motivated and engaged in my work."

20. Do you have any questions for us?

"Yes, I do. Can you tell me more about the typical customer issues I would be handling? What are the main challenges you expect the customer service team to face in the coming year? How do you support professional development and training for your customer service representatives? Additionally, I'm interested in learning more about your approach to customer feedback and continuous improvement."

Responses from a Professional Nurse
1. **Tell me about yourself.**

"I am a registered nurse with over six years of experience in providing compassionate and comprehensive patient care. I hold a Bachelor of Science in Nursing from Duke University and have worked in various healthcare settings, including hospitals and clinics. I am passionate about patient education and holistic care, aiming to improve health outcomes and patient satisfaction."

2. **Why do you want to work here?**

"I am impressed by your hospital's commitment to patient-centered care and its innovative approach to healthcare. Your emphasis on continuous professional development and team collaboration aligns with my career goals. I am particularly excited about the opportunity to work in your Specialist Trauma Center, where I can apply my skills and contribute to high-quality patient care."

3. What are your strengths?

"My strengths include excellent clinical skills, strong communication abilities, and a compassionate approach to patient care. I am adept at quickly assessing patient needs, developing care plans, and providing effective interventions. Additionally, my ability to work well under pressure and collaborate with multidisciplinary teams ensures comprehensive and coordinated care for patients."

4. What are your weaknesses?

"I can be quite meticulous, which sometimes leads to spending extra time on documentation to ensure accuracy. While this attention to detail is crucial in nursing, I am working on improving my efficiency without compromising the quality of my work."

5. Why are you leaving your current job?

"I have enjoyed my time at my current job and have gained valuable experience, but I am seeking new challenges and opportunities for growth. I am particularly interested in your facility because of its strong reputation and the opportunity to work with a diverse patient population, which will further enhance my skills and knowledge."

6. Where do you see yourself in five years?

"In five years, I see myself as a senior nurse or nurse manager, taking on more leadership responsibilities and continuing to advocate for high-quality patient care. I aim to further my education, possibly pursuing a Nurse Practitioner certification, and contribute to policy and procedural improvements within the healthcare setting."

7. Can you describe a challenging situation and how you handled it?

"During a night shift, I managed a situation where a patient experienced a sudden decline in their condition. I quickly assessed the situation, initiated emergency protocols, and coordinated with the healthcare team to stabilize the patient. My prompt action and effective communication ensured the patient received timely care, which ultimately improved their outcome."

8. **What are your salary expectations?**

"Based on my research and experience, I am expecting a salary in the range of $120,000 to $150,000. However, I am open to discussing this further and am flexible based on the overall compensation package, benefits, and opportunities for professional development."

9. **Why should we hire you?**

"I bring a strong background in patient care, excellent clinical skills, and a compassionate approach that aligns with your organization's values. My ability to work effectively under pressure and collaborate with multidisciplinary teams ensures comprehensive care for patients. I am confident that my experience and dedication will make a positive contribution to your team."

10. Tell me about a time you demonstrated leadership skills.

"As the charge nurse during a particularly busy shift, I coordinated patient care, managed staffing issues, and ensured that all patients received timely attention. I also mentored junior nurses and provided support during critical situations. My leadership helped maintain a high standard of care and fostered a collaborative team environment."

11. How do you handle stress and pressure?

"I handle stress by staying organized and prioritizing my tasks. I use time management techniques to ensure that critical tasks are completed first. Additionally, I practice self-care by engaging in regular exercise, mindfulness activities, and maintaining a healthy work-life balance. These strategies help me stay focused and effective under pressure."

12. What do you know about our facility?

"Your facility is renowned for its commitment to excellence in patient care and innovation in healthcare. I am particularly impressed by your specialized programs in [specific area] and the emphasis on continuous professional development for staff. Your collaborative and patient-centered approach aligns well with my professional values."

13. Tell me about a time you made a mistake. How did you handle it?

"During a shift, I once realized that I had administered the wrong dosage of medication to a patient. I immediately reported the mistake to my supervisor, informed the patient and their family, and monitored the patient closely for any adverse effects. I also reviewed the medication administration process and implemented additional checks to prevent future errors. This experience reinforced the importance of vigilance and transparency in nursing."

14. How do you prioritize your work?

"I prioritize my work by assessing the urgency and importance of each task. I use the SBAR (Situation, Background, Assessment, and Recommendation) method to communicate effectively and ensure that critical patient needs are addressed promptly. I also delegate tasks appropriately and collaborate with the healthcare team to manage workload and ensure comprehensive patient care."

15. What is your greatest professional achievement?

"My greatest professional achievement was leading a quality improvement project that significantly reduced the incidence of hospital-acquired infections in our unit. By implementing evidence-based practices, conducting staff training, and monitoring compliance, we achieved a 40% reduction in infections, which greatly improved patient outcomes and safety."

16. Describe a time when you had to work as part of a team.

"In a multidisciplinary team for a patient with complex needs, I worked closely with doctors, physical therapists, and social workers to develop a comprehensive care plan. We held regular meetings to discuss the patient's progress and adjust the plan as needed. By leveraging each team member's expertise, we provided holistic and effective care that led to significant improvements in the patient's health."

17. How do you handle feedback and criticism?

"I view feedback and criticism as valuable opportunities for growth. I listen carefully, ask clarifying questions if needed, and reflect on how I can improve my practice. For example, after receiving feedback on my bedside manner, I attended a communication skills workshop and incorporated more empathetic and patient-centered approaches into my interactions, which enhanced patient satisfaction."

18. Tell me about a time you had a conflict with a coworker and how you resolved it.

"I once had a disagreement with a coworker about the best approach to a patient's care plan. I suggested we discuss our perspectives and seek input from the rest of the healthcare team. Through open communication and focusing on the patient's best interests, we reached a consensus on the most appropriate care plan and worked together effectively to implement it."

19. What motivates you?

"I am motivated by the opportunity to make a positive impact on patients' lives through compassionate and high-quality care. Seeing patients recover and improve their health outcomes is incredibly rewarding. Continuous learning and professional development also keep me motivated and engaged in my nursing practice."

20. Do you have any questions for us?

"Yes, I do. Can you tell me more about the patient population I would be working with? What are the main challenges you expect the unit to face in the coming year? How do you support professional development and continuing education for your nursing staff? Additionally, I'm interested in learning more about your approach to interdisciplinary collaboration and patient care.

Responses from an Academic

1. Tell me about yourself.

"I hold a Ph.D. in Computing from University of South Alabama and have over eight years of experience in academic research and teaching. My research focuses on Cybersecurity, and I have published several papers in peer-reviewed journals. I am passionate about mentoring students and fostering a collaborative learning environment."

2. Why do you want to work here?

"I am impressed by your institution's commitment to academic excellence and innovation. The interdisciplinary approach and emphasis on research align perfectly with my professional goals. I am particularly excited about the opportunity to collaborate with your distinguished faculty and contribute to your [specific program or department]."

3. What are your strengths?

"One of my key strengths is my ability to conduct rigorous research and effectively communicate findings. I have a strong track record of securing research grants and publishing high-impact papers. Additionally, my passion for teaching and mentoring allows me to inspire and support students in their academic journeys."

4. What are your weaknesses?

"I can be quite detail-oriented, which sometimes leads to spending extra time on certain tasks. While this ensures high-quality work, I have been working on balancing thoroughness with efficiency to meet deadlines more effectively."

5. Why are you leaving your current job?

"I have enjoyed my time at my current institution, but I am seeking new challenges and opportunities for growth. I am particularly interested in your university because of its strong research culture and the potential for interdisciplinary collaboration."

6. Where do you see yourself in five years?

"In five years, I see myself as a tenured professor leading impactful research projects and contributing to the development of innovative curricula. I aim to continue publishing high-quality research and mentoring the next generation of scholars."

7. Can you describe a challenging situation and how you handled it?

"During my postdoctoral research, I faced a challenge when a key experiment did not yield the expected results. I re-evaluated the experimental design, consulted with colleagues, and conducted additional trials. This iterative approach led to new insights and ultimately resulted in a publication that garnered significant attention in our field."

8. What are your salary expectations?

"Based on my research and experience, I am expecting a salary in the range of $65,000 to $95,000. However, I am open to discussing this further and am flexible based on the overall compensation package and opportunities for professional development."

9. Why should we hire you?

"I bring a strong background in [specific area], with a proven track record of research excellence and effective teaching. My experience in securing funding and publishing in top journals demonstrates my ability to contribute to your institution's academic reputation. Additionally, my dedication to student success and collaboration makes me a strong fit for your team."

10. Tell me about a time you demonstrated leadership skills.

"As the lead investigator on a multi-institutional research project, I coordinated efforts between different research teams, managed the budget, and ensured timely progress. My leadership helped secure a significant grant and resulted in several high-impact publications. I also mentored junior researchers and facilitated productive collaborations."

11. How do you handle stress and pressure?

"I handle stress by staying organized and prioritizing my tasks. I break down large projects into manageable steps and set realistic deadlines. Additionally, I find that maintaining a healthy work-life balance through regular exercise and hobbies helps me stay focused and productive under pressure."

12. What do you know about our institution?

"Your institution is renowned for its commitment to research and academic excellence. I am particularly impressed by your [specific program or initiative] and the collaborative environment you foster. Your recent initiatives in Science and Technology align well with my research interests and professional goals in addressing pressing challenges in Computing and Brain Resilience."

13. Tell me about a time you made a mistake. How did you handle it?

"During a research project, I realized I had miscalculated a key variable in my data analysis. I immediately notified my team, corrected the error, and re-analyzed the data. I also implemented a more rigorous review process to prevent similar mistakes in the future. This experience taught me the importance of diligence and transparency in research."

14. How do you prioritize your work?

"I prioritize my work by assessing the urgency and importance of each task. I use project management tools to keep track of deadlines and milestones and regularly review my priorities to ensure alignment with my research and teaching goals. Effective time management and clear communication with colleagues and students are key to my process."

15. What is your greatest professional achievement?

"My greatest professional achievement was securing a major research grant for my work on Cybersecurity. This grant not only funded my research but also supported several graduate students. The findings from this project have been published in top journals and have had a significant impact on our field."

16. Describe a time when you had to work as part of a team.

"In a collaborative research project with multiple universities, I worked closely with a diverse team of researchers and students. We held regular meetings to discuss progress, share insights, and address challenges. By leveraging each team member's expertise, we were able to produce a comprehensive study that was well-received in the academic community."

17. How do you handle feedback and criticism?

"I view feedback and criticism as valuable opportunities for growth. I listen carefully, ask clarifying questions if needed, and reflect on how I can improve. For example, after receiving feedback on my teaching methods, I incorporated more interactive and student-centered approaches, which significantly improved student engagement and learning outcomes."

18. Tell me about a time you had a conflict with a coworker and how you resolved it.

"I once had a disagreement with a colleague about the direction of a joint research project. I suggested we sit down and discuss our perspectives openly. By listening to each other and considering the pros and cons of each approach, we were able to reach a consensus and develop a plan that satisfied both of us and benefited the project."

19. What motivates you?

"I am motivated by the opportunity to advance knowledge in my field and contribute to academic excellence. Seeing the impact of my research and inspiring students to achieve their potential is incredibly rewarding. Continuous learning and collaboration with colleagues also keep me motivated and engaged."

20. Do you have any questions for us?

"Yes, I do. Can you tell me more about the research support and resources available for faculty members? What are the main challenges you expect the department to face in the coming years? How do you support professional development and growth within the institution? Additionally, I'm interested in learning more about the opportunities for interdisciplinary collaboration."

Responses from an Operation Manager
1. Tell me about yourself.

"I have over ten years of experience in operations management, with a focus on optimizing processes, improving efficiency, and enhancing overall business performance. I hold an MBA with a specialization in Operations Management from University of Florida.

Throughout my career, I have successfully led cross-functional teams, managed complex projects, and implemented strategic initiatives that have resulted in significant cost savings and operational improvements."

2. Why do you want to work here?

"I am impressed by your company's commitment to innovation and excellence. Your focus on continuous improvement and sustainability aligns with my professional values. I am particularly excited about the opportunity to contribute to your dynamic team and help drive operational efficiency and growth in a company that is a leader in its industry."

3. What are your strengths?

"My strengths include strategic planning, problem-solving, and leadership. I have a strong ability to analyze complex processes and identify areas for improvement. My experience in managing cross-functional teams and projects has equipped me with excellent communication and collaboration skills, enabling me to drive initiatives that enhance efficiency and productivity."

4. What are your weaknesses?

"I can sometimes be very detail-oriented, which may lead to spending extra time on minor aspects of a project. While this ensures thoroughness, I am working on balancing attention to detail with the need to meet deadlines efficiently by delegating tasks appropriately and focusing on the bigger picture."

5. Why are you leaving your current job?

"I have enjoyed my time at my current company and have gained valuable experience. However, I am seeking new challenges and opportunities for growth. Your company's innovative approach and commitment to operational excellence present the perfect environment for me to apply my skills and further develop my career."

6. Where do you see yourself in five years?

"In five years, I see myself in a senior operations role, such as Director of Operations or Chief Operating Officer, leading strategic initiatives and driving significant improvements across the organization. I aim to leverage my experience and skills to contribute to the long-term success and growth of the company."

7. Can you describe a challenging situation and how you handled it?

"In my previous role, I faced a significant challenge when we needed to overhaul our supply chain processes due to inefficiencies. I led a cross-functional team to analyze the existing processes, identify bottlenecks, and implement new strategies. Through effective communication, collaboration, and continuous monitoring, we reduced lead times by 25% and achieved substantial cost savings."

8. What are your salary expectations?

"Based on my research and experience, I am expecting a salary in the range of $100,000 to $120,000. However, I am open to discussing this further and am flexible based on the overall compensation package, benefits, and opportunities for growth within the company."

9. Why should we hire you?

"I bring a strong background in operations management with a proven track record of optimizing processes, reducing costs, and improving efficiency. My strategic planning skills, leadership abilities, and dedication to continuous improvement make me a valuable asset. I am confident that my experience and passion for operational excellence will contribute positively to your company's success."

10. Tell me about a time you demonstrated leadership skills.

"As the operations manager during a company-wide system upgrade, I led a team of 20 employees to ensure a smooth transition. I coordinated training sessions, managed timelines, and addressed any issues promptly. My leadership helped the team stay focused and motivated, resulting in a successful upgrade that improved our operational efficiency significantly."

11. How do you handle stress and pressure?

"I handle stress by staying organized and prioritizing my tasks. I use project management tools to keep track of deadlines and milestones. Additionally, I practice regular physical exercise and mindfulness techniques to maintain a healthy work-life balance. These strategies help me stay focused and perform effectively under pressure."

12. What do you know about our company?

"Your company is known for its innovation and commitment to excellence in [industry]. I am impressed by your focus on sustainability and continuous improvement. Your recent initiatives in [specific area] demonstrate your leadership in the industry and your dedication to operational efficiency and customer satisfaction."

13. Tell me about a time you made a mistake. How did you handle it?

"During a project rollout, I overlooked a critical stakeholder's input, which led to a delay in implementation. I immediately took responsibility, informed my team and the stakeholders, and scheduled an urgent meeting to address the oversight. By collaborating and incorporating the necessary changes, we were able to get the project back on track. This experience taught me the importance of thorough stakeholder engagement and communication."

14. How do you prioritize your work?

"I prioritize my work by assessing the urgency and importance of each task. I use project management tools to organize and track progress. I also set clear goals and deadlines and regularly review my priorities to ensure alignment with company objectives. Effective delegation and communication with my team are key to managing workload efficiently."

15. What is your greatest professional achievement?

"My greatest professional achievement was leading a lean transformation initiative that resulted in a 30% reduction in production costs and a 20% increase in efficiency. By implementing lean methodologies, training employees, and fostering a culture of continuous improvement, we achieved significant operational improvements that had a lasting positive impact on the organization."

16. Describe a time when you had to work as part of a team.

"In a project to streamline our logistics operations, I worked closely with the logistics, IT, and finance teams. We conducted process mapping sessions and collaborated to identify inefficiencies. By leveraging each team member's expertise, we developed and implemented new processes that improved delivery times and reduced costs. Our collaborative efforts led to a 15% improvement in overall logistics performance."

17. How do you handle feedback and criticism?

"I view feedback and criticism as valuable opportunities for growth. I listen carefully, ask clarifying questions if needed, and reflect on how I can improve. For example, after receiving feedback on my approach to team meetings, I adjusted my communication style to be more inclusive and transparent, which improved team collaboration and morale."

18. Tell me about a time you had a conflict with a coworker and how you resolved it.

"I had a disagreement with a coworker about the best approach to a process improvement initiative. I suggested we discuss our perspectives openly and seek input from the team. By fostering a respectful and constructive dialogue, we were able to reach a compromise that incorporated the best aspects of both approaches. This collaboration led to a successful implementation and strengthened our working relationship."

19. What motivates you?

"I am motivated by the opportunity to drive improvements and make a positive impact on the organization. Solving complex operational challenges and seeing the tangible results of efficiency and productivity enhancements is incredibly rewarding. Continuous learning and professional development also keep me motivated and engaged in my work."

20. Do you have any questions for us?

"Yes, I do. Can you tell me more about the key challenges your operations team is currently facing? What are the main priorities for the operations department in the coming year? How do you support professional development and continuous improvement for your operations staff? Additionally, I'm interested in learning more about your approach to innovation and process optimization."

www.ingramcontent.com/pod-product-compliance
Lightning Source LLC
Chambersburg PA
CBHW071924210526
45479CB00002B/543